All Scripture references taken from the KJV of the Holy Bible, unless otherwise indicated.

HEALING THE FATHER-SON WOUND: A Prayer Manual for Breaking Word Curses, Restoring Identity and Reclaiming Destiny

by Dr. Marlene Miles

Freshwater Press 2025

Freshwaterpress9@gmail.com

ISBN: 978-1-967860-90-6

Paperback Version

Copyright 2025, Dr. Marlene Miles

All rights reserved. No part of this book may be reproduced, distributed, or transmitted by any means or in any means including photocopying, recording or other electronic or mechanical methods without prior written permission of the publisher except in the case of brief publications or critical reviews.

Table of Contents

DEDICATION 6
PREFACE 7
INTRODUCTION 8
HOW TO USE THIS MANUAL 10
DAY 1 — Opening Prayer of Positioning .11
REFLECTION PAGES 12
DAY 2 — Renouncing Negative Words & Word-Curses 14
REFLECTION PAGES 15
DAY 3 — Breaking the Words of the Father 17
REFLECTION PAGES 18
DAY 4 — Healing Identity & Restoring Worth 20
REFLECTION PAGES 21
DAY 5 — Forgiveness of the Father 23
REFLECTION PAGES 24
DAY 6 — Separating Honor From Harm .. 26
REFLECTION PAGES 27
DAY 7 — Blessing Yourself & Your Future 29
REFLECTION PAGES 30

DAY 8 — Breaking Household Idolatry ...32

REFLECTION PAGES 33

DAY 9 — Intercession for the Child-Version of You 35

REFLECTION PAGES 36

DAY 10 — Elevating the Good.................38

REFLECTION PAGES 39

DAY 11 — Blessing the Father 41

REFLECTION PAGES 42

DAY 12 — Final Sealing Decrees 44

REFLECTION PAGES 45

DAY 13 — OPENING PRAYER OF POSITIONING..47

REFLECTION PAGES 48

DAY 14 — RENOUNCING NEGATIVE WORDS..50

REFLECTION PAGES 51

DAY 15 — BREAKING THE WORDS OF THE FATHER..53

REFLECTION PAGES 54

DAY 16 — HEALING MY SELF-WORTH 56

REFLECTION PAGES 57

DAY 17 — FORGIVING MY FATHER.........59

REFLECTION PAGES 60

DAY 18 — HONOR WITHOUT AGREEMENT
.... 62

REFLECTION PAGES 63

DAY 19 — BLESSING MY FUTURE 65

REFLECTION PAGES 66

DAY 20 — BREAKING HOUSEHOLD IDOLATRY 68

REFLECTION PAGES 69

DAY 21 — HEALING THE CHILD WITHIN . 71

REFLECTION PAGES 72

DAY 22 — REMEMBERING THE GOOD 74

REFLECTION PAGES 75

DAY 23 — BLESSING MY FATHER 77

REFLECTION PAGES 78

DAY 24 — SEALING PRAYER 80

REFLECTION PAGES 81

Prayer To Break Soul Ties With Pain 83

BLESSING FOR THE READER 86

REFLECTION PAGES 87

Dear Reader 89

Prayer Books by this Author 90

Relationship Books by this Author 92
Other Series 99

DEDICATION

This manual is dedicated to every son and daughter who grew up longing for the blessing of their father.
May the Father of Lights heal, restore, and rewrite your story with love.

HEALING THE FATHER~SON WOUND

A Prayer Manual for Breaking Word-Curses Restoring Identity and Reclaiming Destiny

PREFACE

The father carries authority, spoken or unspoken, gentle or harsh, present or absent. Many of us inherited wounds not from deliberate malice but from brokenness passed down through generations. This manual is designed to lead you through healing, release, forgiveness, breaking word-curses, and restoration of identity in Christ.

Through the Blood of Jesus, the voice of the Heavenly Father now speaks louder than every earthly voice.

INTRODUCTION

There are wounds only a father can give...
and wounds only the Heavenly Father can
heal.

The words of a father carry tremendous
spiritual weight.
They can shape identity—or fracture it.
They can bless—or bind.
They can plant confidence—or cultivate
fear.

Whether your father was present or absent,
affirming or harsh, gentle or hurting,
himself,—this manual is designed to help
you:

Break the power of negative father-spoken
words

Heal the father-identity wound

Rebuild your God-given identity

Release forgiveness

Bless your father without agreeing with his
brokenness

Embrace the voice of your true Father in
heaven

These prayers are crafted for daily devotion, emotional healing, and spiritual deliverance.
Pray them slowly.
Pray them intentionally.
Pray them with expectation.

Your Father in heaven hears.
He heals.
He restores.
He rewrites stories.

HOW TO USE THIS MANUAL

Pray slowly and prayerfully.

Speak each prayer aloud when possible.

Pause and journal reflections when the Holy Spirit reveals wounds.

Repeat sections as needed.

Healing is many times, layered, not instantly or all at once.

Keep this devotional close; it is designed to travel with you.

DAY 1 — Opening Prayer of Positioning

Lord, have mercy on me and thank You for the opportunity to come before

You.
I silence all judgment, revenge, and retaliation from my heart, but I condemn every condemning, judgmental, evil, limiting, biting, defeating, and hurtful word spoken over me or my children.
I stand in the authority of Isaiah 54:17. Thank You that the Blood of Jesus speaks a better Word. In the Name of Jesus. Amen.

REFLECTION PAGES

(For journaling after each day)

What did the Holy Spirit reveal to me today?

What memories surfaced?

What identity lies did I release?

What truths did God speak to me?

_____
_____
_____

What changes do I feel in my heart?

_____
_____
_____
_____

DAY 2 — Renouncing Negative Words & Word-Curses

Prayer of Renunciation

Lord, I renounce and denounce every negative or careless word spoken over me

or my children.
Forgive me for any words I spoke over others that were destructive.
I withdraw them and place them under the Blood of Jesus.

I break the power of every destructive word.
I cancel its assignment.
I forgive those who spoke them.
And I bless them.
I receive Your truth: I am blessed, chosen, redeemed, and loved.
In Jesus' Name, Amen.

REFLECTION PAGES

(For journaling after each day)

What did the Holy Spirit reveal to me today?

_____

_____

_____
_____
_____
_____

What memories surfaced?

_____
_____
_____
_____
_____

What identity lies did I release?

_____
_____
_____
_____

What truths did God speak to me?

_____

_____

_____

What changes do I feel in my heart?

_____

_____

_____

_____

_____

DAY 3 — Breaking the Words of the Father

Prayer Against Father-Spoken Words

In the Name of Jesus Christ,
I break every assignment of every demon or unclean spirit sent to enforce negative words spoken by my natural father or any

father-figure.
I break evil soul ties connected to pain, limitation, failure, and darkness.
I reject every identity spoken over me that is not from God.

Lord, remove any unbelief that keeps me from receiving Your truth.
Thank You that I am fearfully and wonderfully made—Your masterpiece.
Amen.

REFLECTION PAGES

(For journaling after each day)

What did the Holy Spirit reveal to me today?

_____

_____

_____

_____

What memories surfaced?

What identity lies did I release?

What truths did God speak to me?

What changes do I feel in my heart?

DAY 4 — Healing Identity & Restoring Worth

Identity Prayer

Lord, renew my identity in You.
Break every belief that says I was a
mistake, not enough, unworthy, or cursed.

Thank You that I am created on purpose and with purpose.

> In the Name of Jesus. Amen.

REFLECTION PAGES

(For journaling after each day)

What did the Holy Spirit reveal to me today?

_____

_____

_____

_____

What memories surfaced?

What identity lies did I release?

What truths did God speak to me?

What changes do I feel in my heart?

DAY 5 — Forgiveness of the Father

Lord, I forgive my father for every hurtful word he spoke—
every vain imagination, every careless phrase.
Show Your mercy and lovingkindness to him.
I choose blessing instead of bitterness.
Restore his soul. Shepherd his heart.
In Jesus' Name. Amen.

REFLECTION PAGES

(For journaling after each day)

What did the Holy Spirit reveal to me today?

_____

_____

_____

_____

_____

What memories surfaced?

_____
_____
_____
_____
_____

What identity lies did I release?

_____
_____
_____
_____

What truths did God speak to me?

_____
_____
_____

What changes do I feel in my heart?

_____

_____

_____

_____

_____

DAY 6 — Separating Honor From Harm

Dad, I love and honor you, but I reject every word you spoke that was rooted in fear, limitation, or brokenness.
I reject the belief that I cannot live without you or succeed without your approval.
I embrace God's truth:
I am on the Lord's side.
I am created for good works.
I will succeed.
I will rise.

I will bring God glory.
In the Name of Jesus. Amen.

REFLECTION PAGES

(For journaling after each day)

What did the Holy Spirit reveal to me today?

_____
_____
_____
_____
_____
_____
_____

What memories surfaced?

_____
_____
_____
_____
_____
_____

What identity lies did I release?

_____
_____
_____
_____
_____

What truths did God speak to me?

_____
_____
_____
_____
_____

What changes do I feel in my heart?

_____

_____

_____

_____

DAY 7 — Blessing Yourself & Your Future

I can marry as the Lord wills.
I can build a home.
I can prosper without sorrow.
I can live, move, and have my being in Christ.
Every blessing God has for me, I receive.

    In the Name of Jesus. Amen.

REFLECTION PAGES

(For journaling after each day)

What did the Holy Spirit reveal to me today?

_____
_____
_____
_____
_____

What memories surfaced?

_____
_____

_____

_____

_____

_____

_____

What identity lies did I release?

_____

_____

_____

_____

What truths did God speak to me?

_____

_____

_____

_____

What changes do I feel in my heart?

DAY 8 — Breaking Household Idolatry

In the Name of Jesus, I condemn and reject every idolatry in my father's house. Every pattern, every expectation, every bondage—be broken now.

In the Name of Jesus. Amen.

REFLECTION PAGES

(For journaling after each day)

What did the Holy Spirit reveal to me today?

_____
_____
_____
_____
_____
_____
_____

What memories surfaced?

_____
_____

_____
_____
_____
_____

What identity lies did I release?

_____
_____
_____
_____

What truths did God speak to me?

_____
_____
_____
_____

What changes do I feel in my heart?

_____
_____

DAY 9 — Intercession for the Child-Version of You

Lord, step into every moment of my childhood where harmful words were spoken.
Raise up a standard.
Let every curse fall to the ground as dust and be no more.

    In the Name of Jesus. Amen.

REFLECTION PAGES

(For journaling after each day)

What did the Holy Spirit reveal to me today?

_____
_____
_____
_____
_____
_____

What memories surfaced?

_____
_____
_____
_____

What identity lies did I release?

What truths did God speak to me?

What changes do I feel in my heart?

DAY 10 — Elevating the Good

Let my father's good words—words of
life, wisdom, joy, and honor—
be magnified in my memory.
Let all others fade away.

    In the Name of Jesus. Amen.

REFLECTION PAGES

(For journaling after each day)

What did the Holy Spirit reveal to me today?

_____
_____
_____
_____
_____
_____
_____

What memories surfaced?

_____
_____
_____
_____
_____

What identity lies did I release?

_____

_____

_____

What truths did God speak to me?

_____

_____

_____

What changes do I feel in my heart?

_____

_____

_____

DAY 11 — Blessing the Father

Dad, may the Lord bless you and keep you.
May His face shine upon you and give you peace.
May the meditations of your heart bless the Lord.
May His shalom be yours."\

    In the Name of Jesus. Amen.

REFLECTION PAGES

(For journaling after each day)

What did the Holy Spirit reveal to me today?

_____
_____
_____
_____
_____
_____

What memories surfaced?

_____
_____
_____
_____
_____

What identity lies did I release?

_____
_____
_____
_____

What truths did God speak to me?

_____
_____
_____
_____

What changes do I feel in my heart?

_____
_____
_____

DAY 12 — Final Sealing Decrees

I seal every prayer, decree, and declaration across every dimension of my life in Jesus' Name.

I seal them with the Blood of Jesus and the Holy Spirit of Promise.

Any retaliation against me or anyone praying these prayers—*backfire without mercy*, in Jesus' Name.

AMEN.

REFLECTION PAGES

(For journaling after each day)

What did the Holy Spirit reveal to me today?

_____
_____
_____
_____
_____
_____

What memories surfaced?

_____
_____
_____
_____
_____

What identity lies did I release?

What truths did God speak to me?

What changes do I feel in my heart?

DAY 13 — OPENING PRAYER OF POSITIONING

Lord, have mercy on me.
Thank You for allowing me to come before You in prayer.
I silence all desire for retaliation, revenge, or judgment.
But I condemn every condemning, judgmental, evil, limiting, biting, defeating, or hurtful word spoken over me or my children.

I stand in the authority of Isaiah 54:17: *"No weapon formed against me shall prosper, and every tongue that rises against me in judgment I shall condemn."*

Thank You, Father, that the Bood of Jesus speaks a better Word.
In the Name of Jesus. Amen.

REFLECTION PAGES

(For journaling after each day)

What did the Holy Spirit reveal to me today?

_____
_____
_____
_____
_____
_____

What memories surfaced?

_____
_____
_____
_____
_____
_____
_____

What identity lies did I release?

_____
_____
_____
_____
_____

What truths did God speak to me?

_____
_____
_____
_____
_____

What changes do I feel in my heart?

_____
_____
_____
_____
_____

DAY 14 — RENOUNCING NEGATIVE WORDS

Lord, I renounce and denounce every negative, careless, destructive, or limiting word spoken over me or my children. Forgive me for any words I spoke in frustration, fear, or anger that harmed others.
I withdraw those words and place them under the blood of Jesus.

I break their power.
I cancel their assignment.
I forgive those who spoke them.
I bless them.
I receive Your truth instead:
I am chosen, redeemed, and deeply loved.
In Jesus' Name. Amen.

REFLECTION PAGES

(For journaling after each day)

What did the Holy Spirit reveal to me today?

___

___

___

___

___

___

What memories surfaced?

___

___

___

___

___

___

What identity lies did I release?

_____
_____
_____
_____
_____

What truths did God speak to me?

_____
_____
_____
_____

What changes do I feel in my heart?

_____
_____
_____
_____

DAY 15 — BREAKING THE WORDS OF THE FATHER

In the Name of Jesus, I break every assignment of every demon or unclean spirit sent to enforce negative words spoken by my natural father or any father-figure.

I break ungodly soul ties to pain, failure, fear, limitation, sabotaging patterns, and emotional bondage.
I reject every identity spoken over me that is not from You, Lord.

Thank You that I am fearfully and wonderfully made.
Amen.

REFLECTION PAGES

(For journaling after each day)

What did the Holy Spirit reveal to me today?

_____
_____
_____
_____
_____
_____
_____

What memories surfaced?

_____
_____
_____
_____
_____
_____
_____

What identity lies did I release?

_____
_____
_____
_____

What truths did God speak to me?

_____
_____
_____
_____

What changes do I feel in my heart?

_____
_____
_____
_____

DAY 16 — HEALING MY SELF-WORTH

Lord, remove every belief that says:
"I am not enough."
"I am a mistake."
"I don't matter."
"I am cursed."
"I cannot succeed."

I declare:
I was created on purpose and with purpose.
I am Your masterpiece.
I am who You say I am.

      In the Name of Jesus. Amen.

REFLECTION PAGES

(For journaling after each day)

What did the Holy Spirit reveal to me today?

_____
_____
_____
_____
_____
_____
_____

What memories surfaced?

_____
_____
_____
_____
_____
_____
_____

What identity lies did I release?

_____
_____
_____

What truths did God speak to me?

_____
_____
_____

What changes do I feel in my heart?

_____
_____
_____
_____
_____

DAY 17 — FORGIVING MY FATHER

Lord, I forgive my father for every hurtful word he spoke—
every careless comment,
every fear-based warning,
every angry outburst,
every silence that felt like rejection.

    Show him mercy and lovingkindness.
I choose blessing instead of bitterness. In the Name of Jesus. Amen.

REFLECTION PAGES

(For journaling after each day)

What did the Holy Spirit reveal to me today?

_____
_____
_____
_____
_____

What memories surfaced?

_____
_____
_____
_____
_____
_____
_____

What identity lies did I release?

_____
_____
_____
_____
_____

What truths did God speak to me?

_____
_____
_____
_____
_____

What changes do I feel in my heart?

_____
_____
_____
_____
_____

DAY 18 — HONOR WITHOUT AGREEMENT

Dad, I love and honor you.
But I reject every word you spoke rooted in fear, limitation, discouragement, anger, or brokenness.

I reject any belief that I cannot survive, thrive, or succeed without you.
I reject every negative identity and every limiting expectation.

I embrace God's truth:
I am created for good works.
I will rise.
I will prosper.
I will glorify God.
In the Name of Jesus. Amen.

REFLECTION PAGES

(For journaling after each day)

What did the Holy Spirit reveal to me today?

_____

_____

_____

_____

_____

_____

_____

What memories surfaced?

_____

_____

_____

_____

_____

_____

What identity lies did I release?

_____
_____
_____
_____

What truths did God speak to me?

_____
_____
_____
_____

What changes do I feel in my heart?

_____
_____
_____
_____
_____

DAY 19 — BLESSING MY FUTURE

I declare in the Name of Jesus:

I will marry as the Lord wills.

I will build a home.

I will prosper without sorrow.

I can succeed in everything God has assigned to me.

I live, move, and have my being in Christ.

Every blessing God has for me—I receive it.

> In the Name of Jesus. Amen.

REFLECTION PAGES

(For journaling after each day)

What did the Holy Spirit reveal to me today?

_____
_____
_____
_____
_____
_____

What memories surfaced?

_____
_____
_____
_____
_____
_____
_____

What identity lies did I release?

_____
_____
_____
_____

What truths did God speak to me?

_____
_____
_____
_____

What changes do I feel in my heart?

_____
_____
_____
_____

DAY 20 — BREAKING HOUSEHOLD IDOLATRY

In the Name of Jesus, I reject and renounce
every idolatry in my father's house—
every unspoken expectation,
every destructive pattern,
every cultural bondage,
every generational curse.

Lord, cleanse the foundation.
Reset my lineage.
Restore my inheritance.

> In the Name of Jesus. Amen.

REFLECTION PAGES

(For journaling after each day)

What did the Holy Spirit reveal to me today?

_____

_____

_____

_____

_____

_____

_____

What memories surfaced?

_____

_____

_____

_____

_____

_____

What identity lies did I release?

_____
_____
_____
_____

What truths did God speak to me?

_____
_____
_____

What changes do I feel in my heart?

_____
_____
_____
_____

DAY 21 — HEALING THE CHILD WITHIN

Lord, step into every moment of my childhood where destructive words were spoken over me—
moments my father did not protect me from,
moments he didn't know how to respond to,
moments he wasn't present for.

Raise up a standard now.
Let every curse fall to the ground as dust.
Let every wound be filled with Your love.

      In the Name of Jesus. Amen.

REFLECTION PAGES

(For journaling after each day)

What did the Holy Spirit reveal to me today?

_____
_____
_____
_____
_____
_____
_____

What memories surfaced?

_____
_____
_____
_____
_____
_____

What identity lies did I release?

_____
_____
_____
_____
_____

What truths did God speak to me?

_____
_____
_____
_____
_____

What changes do I feel in my heart?

_____
_____
_____
_____
_____

DAY 22 — REMEMBERING THE GOOD

Lord, magnify the good.
Elevate every kind word, every wise lesson, every moment of joy my father gave.
Let those memories be amplified.
Let the painful ones fade into silence.

    In the Name of Jesus. Amen.

REFLECTION PAGES

(For journaling after each day)

What did the Holy Spirit reveal to me today?

_____
_____
_____
_____
_____
_____
_____

What memories surfaced?

_____
_____
_____
_____
_____
_____
_____

What identity lies did I release?

_____
_____
_____
_____
_____

What truths did God speak to me?

_____
_____
_____
_____
_____

What changes do I feel in my heart?

_____
_____
_____
_____
_____

DAY 23 — BLESSING MY FATHER

Dad, may the Lord bless you and keep you.
May His face shine upon you and give you peace.
May His goodness rest on your life.
May your heart be healed, renewed, and restored.
May God's shalom surround you.

      In the Name of Jesus. Amen.

REFLECTION PAGES

(For journaling after each day)

What did the Holy Spirit reveal to me today?

_____
_____
_____
_____
_____

What memories surfaced?

_____
_____
_____
_____
_____

What identity lies did I release?

_____

_____

_____

_____

_____

What truths did God speak to me?

_____

_____

_____

_____

_____

What changes do I feel in my heart?

_____

_____

_____

_____

_____

DAY 24 — SEALING PRAYER

I seal every prayer, decree, and declaration across every dimension of my life in Jesus' Name.

I seal them with the Blood of Jesus and the Holy Spirit of Promise.

Any retaliation against me or anyone praying these prayers—backfire without mercy, in Jesus' Name.

AMEN.

REFLECTION PAGES

(For journaling after each day)

What did the Holy Spirit reveal to me today?

_____
_____
_____
_____
_____
_____

What memories surfaced?

_____
_____
_____
_____
_____
_____

What identity lies did I release?

_____
_____
_____
_____
_____

What truths did God speak to me?

_____
_____
_____
_____

What changes do I feel in my heart?

_____
_____
_____
_____

Prayer To Break Soul Ties With Pain

Lord,
Some of us didn't just survive pain —
we attached to it.
We learned through it.
We shaped ourselves around it.
We carried it like it was normal.

But today, Lord,
I break every soul tie I have with pain.

Every part of me that bonded with:

- rejection
- hurt
- disappointment
- silence
- emotional neglect
- ridicule
- instability
- loneliness
- being the strong one

- being the overlooked one
- being the responsible one
- being the peacekeeper

I release it now.

Lord, detach me from the pain that raised me.
Detangle me from the sorrow that shaped me.
Separate me from the identity formed through wounds.
Unhook me from the survival patterns that feel like personality.

I break agreement with:

- "This is just how I am."
- "This is all I know."
- "This is who I'll always be."

No more.
Not today.
Not anymore.

I am tied to healing now.
I am bound to restoration now.
I am connected to wholeness now.

In Jesus' Name, Amen.

(This prayer shared from: **Healing the Sibling & Relative Wound Prayer Manual**
https://a.co/d/iZGi6kt

BLESSING FOR THE READER

May the Father rewrite your story with tenderness.
May His love fill every place where earthly fathers failed.
May His voice become the loudest in your life.
May you rise into your destiny whole, healed, strengthened, and restored.
In Jesus' Name—Amen.

REFLECTION PAGES

(For journaling after each day)

What did the Holy Spirit reveal to me today?

_____
_____
_____
_____
_____

What memories surfaced?

_____
_____
_____
_____
_____
_____

What identity lies did I release?

_____
_____
_____
_____
_____

What truths did God speak to me?

_____
_____
_____
_____
_____

What changes do I feel in my heart?

_____
_____
_____
_____
_____

Dear Reader

      Thank you for acquiring, reading and praying with the prayer manual.

I pray the Lord has richly blessed you and if you are not suddenly delivered, may the Lord do His perfect work in you in His timing by His Grace and your own faith. Be healed. Be made whole. In Jesus' Name, Amen.

 Shalom,

Dr. Marlene Miles

Prayer Books by this Author

Prayer Manuals

SOUL TIE Prayer Manual (The)

MAD at DADDY Prayer Manual

Healing the Sibling & Relative Wound Prayer Manual

Healing the Father-Son Wound Prayer Manual
https://a.co/d/iZGi6kt

Prayers Against Barrenness: *For Success in Business and Life*

Breaking Curses of the Mother

Fruit of the Womb: *Prayers Against Barrenness*

Beauty Curses, *Warfare Prayers Against*
https://a.co/d/5Xlc20M

Courts of Marriage: Prayers for Marriage in the Courts of Heaven *(prayerbook)*
https://a.co/d/cNAdgAq

Courtroom Warfare @ Midnight *(prayerbook)*
https://a.co/d/5fc7Qdp

Relationship Books by this Author

200 RED FLAGS: THE TRACK IS NOT SAFE How to spot red flags in relationships, especially in dating and romantic connections.
https://a.co/d/ckyuqmb

Also, the **RED FLAGS** Workbook. Full size, ample room to write. Have a RED FLAG party with your friends and conquer relationship problems.

<u>**WE GET ALONG, *RIGHT?* Compatibility Reality for Couples**</u>

Companion Workbook: **WE GET ALONG, RIGHT? *The Workbook for Couples Who Think They Do***

Relationship-related Prayerbooks by this author

While most books by this author have prayer points either throughout the book or at the end, there are some books that are only prayers. You just open up the book and pray.

Prayers Against Barrenness: *For Success in Business and Life*

Fruit of the Womb: *Prayers Against Barrenness*

Already Married in the Spirit: *Why You May Not Be Married in the Natural*
https://a.co/d/gVSzfQ2

Anti-Marriage, *The Spirit of*
https://a.co/d/fEKrHFu

Backstabbers https://a.co/d/gi8iBxf

Barrenness, *Prayers Against*
https://a.co/d/feUltIs

Battlefield of Marriage, *The*

Blindsided: *Has the Old Man Bewitched You?*
https://a.co/d/5O2fLLR

Break Free from Collective Captivity

Broken Spirits & Dry Bones

By Means of a Whorish Father
https://a.co/d/hYlfR8b

Casting Down Imaginations

DANGERS OF SEX (The)
https://a.co/d/d3dqoMk

Deliverance Journal

https://a.co/d/72UEUpt *Freshwater Journals*

Devil Loves Trauma, *The*

Devil Weapons: Unforgiveness, Bitterness,…

Dream Defilement

Evil Touch

Fantasy Spirit Spouse
https://a.co/d/hW7oYbX

FAT Demons (The): *Breaking Demonic Curses*
https://a.co/d/4kP8wV1

got LOVE? Verses for Life

Has My Soul Been Sold?
https://a.co/d/dyB8hhA

Hidden Sins: Hidden Iniquity

https://a.co/d/4Mth0wa

Level the Playing Field https://a.co/d/9rdIVtl

Love Breaks Your Heart

Made Perfect In Love

Marriage Ed. Rules of Engagement & Marriage

Made Perfect in Love

Men Shall Dream https://a.co/d/eYWYdFy

Money Hunters: Beware of Those

Players Gonna Play

Second Marriage, Third--, *Any Marriage*

https://a.co/d/6m6GN4N

Seducing Spirits: Idolatry & Whoredoms

https://a.co/d/4Jq4WEs

Six Men Short: What Has Happened to all the Men?

Sleep Afflictions & Really Bad Dreams
https://a.co/d/f8sDmgv

Too Many Wives: *Why You Have Lady Problems*

Tormenting Spirits   https://a.co/d/dAogEJf

Unbreak My Heart: *Don't Let Me Die*

Unseen Life, *The*

Why Do I Keep Meeting the Same Guy?

https://a.co/d/0BcAWmW

WTH? Get Me Out of This Hell

https://a.co/d/a7WBGJh

>Unauthorized Use: This Could Be Why You Are Not Married Yet
>https://a.co/d/edro52M
>
>Unbreak My Heart: *Don't Let Me Die*

 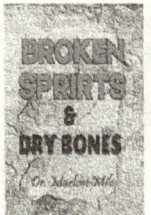 

Other Series
Spirit Spouse books

https://a.co/d/9VehDSo

https://a.co/d/97sKOwm

Battlefield of Marriage, The

https://a.co/d/eUDzizO

Players Gonna Play

https://a.co/d/2hzGw3N

***Sent* Spirit Spouse** (can someone send you a spirit spouse? This book is not yet released.)

The Wilderness Romance *(series)* This series is about conducting a Godly relationship and marriage with someone who is a Wilderness person. It is about how to recognize it and navigate through it. These books are about how not to get caught up in such.

- *The Social Wilderness*
- *The Sexual Wilderness*
- *The Spiritual Wilderness*

www.ingramcontent.com/pod-product-compliance
Lightning Source LLC
Chambersburg PA
CBHW051348040426
42453CB00007B/461